NAILED IT!

Extreme

KITE
SURFING

Virginia Loh-Hagan

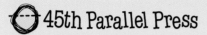
45th Parallel Press

Published in the United States of America by Cherry Lake Publishing
Ann Arbor, Michigan
www.cherrylakepublishing.com

Content Adviser: Liv Williams, Editor, www.iLivExtreme.com
Reading Adviser: Marla Conn, ReadAbility, Inc.
Photo Credits: ©EpicStockMedia/Shutterstock.com, cover, 1; ©Mai Techaphan/Shutterstock.com, 5; ©Mai Techaphan/Shutterstock.com, 7; ©Robert Hardholt/Shutterstock.com,8; ©Erlucho/istockphoto.com, 11; ©Ohrim/Shutterstock.com, 13; ©War Archive/Alamy, 15; ©EpicStockMedia/Thinkstock.com, 17; ©Inc/Shutterstock.com, 19; ©Trevor Waters/Western Mail and Echo Copyright/Newscom, 20; ©Inyrdreams/Dreamstime.com, 23; ©Ohrim/Shutterstock.com, 25; ©Louise Murray/Alamy, 27; ©Mai Techaphan/Shutterstock.com, 28; ©Trusjom/Shutterstock.com, multiple interior pages; ©Kues/Shutterstock.com, multiple interior pages

45th Parallel Press is an imprint of Cherry Lake Publishing.

Library of Congress Cataloging-in-Publication Data

Loh-Hagan, Virginia.
  Extreme kite surfing / Virginia Loh-Hagan.
      pages cm. -- (Nailed It!)
  Includes bibliographical references and index.
  ISBN 978-1-63470-019-1 (hardcover) -- ISBN 978-1-63470-073-3 (pdf) -- ISBN 978-1-63470-046-7 (paperback)
-- ISBN 978-1-63470-100-6 (ebook)
 1. Kite surfing--Juvenile literature. 2. Extreme sports--Juvenile literature. 3. ESPN X-Games--Juvenile literature.
I. Title.

 GV840.K49L65 2015
 797.3--dc23

                              2015006301

ABOUT THE AUTHOR

Dr. Virginia Loh-Hagan is an author, university professor, former classroom teacher, and curriculum designer. She loves kites because they're pretty. She lives in San Diego with her very tall husband and very naughty dogs. To learn more about her, visit www.virginialoh.com.

Table of Contents

Chasing the Wind and Waves

Who is Kevin Langeree? Who is Aaron Hadlow? What do kite surfers chase? What is extreme kite surfing? What do you need in order to kite surf?

Kevin Langeree kite surfs anywhere. He travels around the world.

He went to Alaska. He kite surfed on **icebergs**! An iceberg is a large, floating block of ice. He said, "I saw the perfect cliff to jump off … I don't think there are many people who have jumped out of an iceberg." Langeree jumped from icebergs. He kite surfed in cold waters. He did tricks in the air.

Langeree chases wind. He also chases waves. Kite surfers look for the best places to kite surf.

Kite surfers chase their goals. Aaron Hadlow **landed**, or achieved, the first 900. It's the first time it's been done. A 900 is two and a half turns in the air. He practiced this trick for months.

Kevin Langeree is known as "The Flying Dutchman." He is from the Netherlands.

Most people focus on height. They think getting big air is extreme. They focus on big jumps. Hadlow prefers tricks. He likes doing flips and rolls. He said, "When you see

Spotlight Biography: Jingyue Chen

Jingyue Chen represents China in kite surfing contests. She is from Pingtan. It is an island in China. It is China's windiest city. In the past, China focused on speed racing. Chen is making freestyle kite surfing more important. She was winning contests by the age of 12. She was crowned the champion of the Kiteboard Tour Asia. She takes kite surfing theory lessons. She trains outdoors. Her coach is Michael Khromykh. He is a famous professional freestyle kite surfer. The Pingtan Kiteboarding Association said, "Most Chinese kite riders hone their game by watching videos. It is rare in China to hire someone to coach freestyle kiteboarding classes." Chen is a kite surfer to watch.

Kite surfers do a lot of tricks in the air.

riders jumping as high as possible and throwing a kite loop in there too, then it gets crazy."

Hadlow loves kite surfing. He said, "There's so much you can do. You can ride waves, jump high, or just cruise around."

Kite surfers need a board with footstraps, a harness, and a kite.

Extreme kite surfing is a style of kiteboarding. Kite surfers ride waves. They use special boards called kiteboards. Kiteboards look like small surfboards.

Kiteboards have **footstraps**. Footstraps keep feet on the board. The **harness** connects kite surfers to kites. A harness has straps. It goes around the waist. Kite surfers handle kites with control bars.

Kite surfers use wind power. The kite drags them across water. They jump waves. They can reach 20 to 40 feet (6 to 12 m) above water. They do tricks.

"Kite surfers ride waves. They use special boards called kiteboards."

Kite Surfing with Style!

Which sports do kite surfing combine? Where do kite surfers surf? What are some types of kite surfing?

Kite surfing combines kite flying, surfing, sailing, and skateboarding. Kite surfers cover more area with kites. They go faster than surfers. They go farther than surfers. They use kites like sails. They copy many skateboarding moves.

Kite surfers surf in water. They can kite surf in the ocean or **inland**. Inland water is big lakes and rivers. There are different types of kite surfing.

Kite surfing on waves is one type. Kite surfers use waves like ramps. Waves help them get air. They do big jumps. They do tricks in the air.

Kite surfing on flat water is another type. Flat water means there aren't many waves. This is called freeriding or blasting. The waves aren't big enough for tricks. Kite surfers blast through a straight line. They go as fast as they can. They do turns and jumps.

Freestyle is another type. Kite surfers do tricks. They jump, slide, and spin. The kite lifts kite surfers in the air. They get

Kite surfers need a big body of water. They need space to get going.

more **hang time**. They have more time in the air. It looks like they're in slow motion. They do amazing tricks.

Marc Jacobs does huge backflips. He said, "I love flying and going big."

NAILED IT!

Advice from the Field: Holding the Kite

The kite's shape comes from tubes pumped full of air. It's like a tire. The kite has to be tough and flexible. It has to be strong enough to survive many crashes. Learning how to hold a kite correctly can save a kite surfer's life. A kite surfer can carry a kite if it is turned upside down. If the kite were right side up, it could lift the kite surfer up in the air. When something goes wrong, kite surfers need to let go of the control bar. The kite will hang out in the air. And the kite surfer will be free to move. If kite surfers don't let go, the kite could pull or drag kite surfers through the water.

Kite surfers zip in and out from the beach. They go at high speed. They add jumps or turns.

From Transportation to Sport

How did kite surfing develop? What is its history? How did surfers help make kite surfing popular?

Kiting has a long history. Kites were used to move people and things. The Chinese used kites in the 13th century. They moved **canoes**. Canoes are little boats. In the 19th century, George Pocock invented big kites. He used the kites as sails. Kites moved carts on land. They moved ships in water. In 1903, Samuel Cody invented man-lifting kites. He crossed the English Channel. The English Channel is a body of water between England and France. He did it with a boat and a kite.

In 1977, Gijsbertus Panhuise used kites for play. He invented kite surfing as a water sport. Early kites were more like **parachutes**. Jumpers use parachutes to slow their fall. They look like balloon tops.

Early kite surfers combined kites with skates and skis. Kite surfers worked to improve their gear.

Kite surfing developed from a form of transportation to a sport.

Extreme Kite Surfing: Know the Lingo

Air time: amount of time spent in the air while jumping

Bail: letting go of the kite's control bar and kicking off the board

Board-offs: taking one or both feet off the board

Brain fart: forgetting the trick midair and crashing in the water

Charlie Browner: kite surfer

Chop: little bumps on the water surface created by wind

Downwinder: kite surfing trip from one place to another that is farther downwind

DP: dawn patrol, an early session

Grab: holding the board with one hand

Inverts: any trick done upside down

Kite loops: looping the kite around 360 degrees while doing a spin

Kitemare: a kite surfing accident, disaster

Lines: strong cords connecting a kite surfer to the kite

Nuking: winds blowing at great speeds

Rigging up: putting things together to go kite surfing

Wipeout: crashing

Surfers helped make kite surfing a popular sport.

The Legaignoux brothers developed modern kite surfing. They invented the first **inflatable** kite. Inflatable means it can be pumped with air. The gear got better. So the sport got better.

Laird Hamilton is a big wave surfer. He made kite surfing popular. He used kites to build speed. He wanted to catch big waves. Many surfers like kite surfing. Sometimes, it's too windy to go surfing. So they go kite surfing instead.

Kite surfing was about big jumps. It was about getting big air. Now it's also about doing extreme tricks.

Breaking Records and Breaking Bones

What did Jesse Richman do? What did the Virgin Kitesurfing Armada do?

Jesse Richman breaks records. He stayed in the air for 22 seconds. And he flies high. One time, a boat **towed**, or pulled, him. He got 790.68 feet (241 m) above ground. He was cut loose from the boat. He flew with his kite. He landed in the flat water. He practiced this trick for a year.

The Virgin Kitesurfing **Armada** broke a record. Virgin is the name of a company. It is owned by Richard Branson. An armada is a large group of boats. They created the largest parade of kite surfers. There were 352 kite surfers.

(The last record was 318 kite surfers.) They sailed together for one **nautical** mile. Nautical is anything to do with sailing.

Richard Branson kite surfed the English Channel. He's the oldest person to do this. He was 61 years old. It took him two tries in 24 hours. His son is Sam Branson. He also kite surfed the English Channel. He broke the speed record. He did it in 2 hours and 18 minutes.

Richard Branson said, "I absolutely love the amazing rush you get when going at high speeds, in high winds."

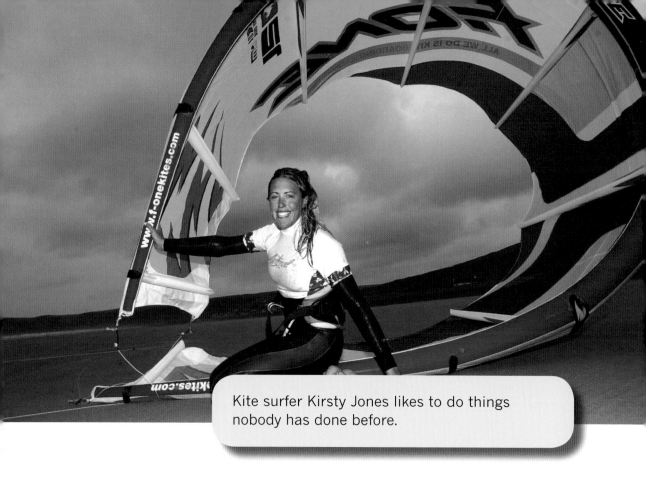

Kite surfer Kirsty Jones likes to do things nobody has done before.

Francisco Lufinha broke a record. He completed the longest kite surfing trip. He kite surfed 307.5 nautical miles (569.5 kilometers). He did this without stopping. He did it in 28 hours and 53 minutes.

Six kite surfers crossed the Atlantic Ocean. This had never been done before. They kite surfed 3,200 nautical miles (5,926 km). It took them 27 days. Each kite surfer took turns. They worked two hours during the day. They worked two hours at night. They didn't stop. They faced some challenges. They saw sharks. They were in bad weather. They worked in the dark.

Getting Your Body Ready!

Francisco Lufinha had to get ready for his kite surfing journey. He followed a strict program. He trained his body. He ate healthy food. He spent many hours kite surfing. He trained in several parts of the country. He also spent 24 hours on a surfboard. He surfed in a swimming pool. He wanted to know how his body would handle standing for a long period of time. He worried about wind. He studied wind charts. He worried about falling asleep on top of his kiteboard. A boat support staff helped him. They provided him with water and food. Lufinha spent a lot of time and energy preparing to break the record.

Kirsty Jones kite surfed across the Irish Sea. She was the first person to do this. She also kite surfed 140 miles (225 km). She did it in nine hours.

Most kite surfing accidents cause bruises and broken ribs. Kite surfers also get cuts on their heads. But some kite surfers die. Wind gets out of control. Kite surfers crash into things.

A kite surfer jumped 100 feet (30.5 m) into the air. A strong wind caught his kite. He was dragged along a beach. He crashed into a metal sign. He was lifted 10 feet (3 m) into the air. He slammed into a building. Then he fell. He landed on the ground.

Some kite surfers suffer the "death loop." Kite lines sometimes loop together. Kite surfers need to release the lines quickly. If they don't, they could fall. Their kites could drag them. Then they could get trapped underwater. They could drown.

"Most kite surfing accidents cause bruises and broken ribs."

Kite surfing can be hard work.

Getting Creative

What are examples of kite surfing stunts? What did Maciek Kozierski do? What did Lewis Crathern do? What did Youri Zoon do?

Kite surfers like to perform stunts.

Maciek Kozierski did more than ride waves. He walked on them. He spent four days on a project. He called it "Miracle." He used his kite to get high speed. He stepped off his kiteboard. He let go of his kite. He walked on water!

He had many challenges. Strong winds made waves too high. Calm water meant there wasn't enough wind. He crashed hard into the water. He crashed more than 50 times. He didn't quit.

Lewis Crathern jumped more than waves. He jumped a **pier**! A pier is a structure from beach out into water. The pier is more than 1,719 feet (524 m). He jumped off a huge wave. He flew through the air. He leaped over the pier.

This stunt was dangerous. He could've crashed into the pier. He worried about not getting high enough. He also worried about his gear failing.

Kite surfers have fun on the water.

Crathern worked hard to get ready. He practiced this stunt for two years. He walked the pier. He measured it. He inspected it. He researched wind charts.

When Extreme Is Too Extreme!

Tropical Storm Fay hit Florida in 2008. Kevin Kearney went kite surfing during this storm. Strong winds took over his kite. He rose into the air. He slammed into the beach. He was dragged along the sand. The kite lifted him into the air again. It slammed him into a building. His harness had emergency clasps. But things happened too fast. He couldn't unhook himself. Kearney hurt his spine. His brain swelled. He broke a rib. He broke an ankle. When he woke up, he had no idea what happened. He eventually remembered. He said he would do it again.

Kite surfing stunts are dangerous. Kite surfers need to be prepared.

Kite surfers have to practice their stunts

Youri Zoon jumped over a small island! It was 120 feet (36 m). He kite surfed in the Pacific Ocean. He traveled 22 miles (35 km) per hour. Strong winds pulled him. He launched 50 feet (15 m) in the air. He jumped over the island in one leap.

He worried about crashing into the beach. He worried

about hitting **shallow** water. Shallow means the water is not deep. He practiced this stunt several times. On his third try, he crashed into a tree.

Zoon said, "Making the jump felt amazing. I got a rush of **adrenaline** as I took off." Adrenaline gives a person more energy.

Kite surfers plan and practice. They create ways to have fun.

"Making the jump felt amazing. I got a rush of adrenaline as I took off."

Did You Know?

- Kite surfing is featured in *Die Another Day.* It is a James Bond movie. James Bond kite surfs on a car hood. He rides a huge wave. He uses a parachute. The computer created this scene. It would be impossible to do this stunt in real life.

- Kite surfers like to go to Luderitz in Namibia. It is in Africa. It is a town by the coast. It has calm waters. It has strong winds. It has the best speed-sailing conditions. Great white sharks swim in the waters. But kite surfers go too fast for a great white shark to catch them!

- Rhyl is a city in the United Kingdom. The city has turned a block of toilets into a kite surfing school. The building will have an office. It will also have a space for training, changing, and drying. It is only 66 feet (20 m) from the beach.

- The International Sailing Federation voted to include kiteboarding in the 2016 Olympics. Then they changed their mind. They voted to include windsurfing instead.

- The military used kites in the U.S. Civil War. Kites were used to send messages.

- *Fen zheng* is the Chinese name for kite. It means "wind harp." Early Chinese kites were used to carry musical instruments.

- The sun's heat takes longer to warm the sea than land. This creates a difference in air pressure. This creates sea breezes.

Consider This!

TAKE A POSITION! Should kite surfing be included in the Olympics? Some people consider it to be too extreme. They think it should be part of the X Games. Other people think that kite surfing should be part of the Olympics. They think that kite surfing deserves more recognition. What do you think? Argue your position with reasons and evidence.

SAY WHAT? Extreme kite surfers have rules. They follow the "Kite High Rule." Kite surfers must keep their lines high or low. They need to avoid crossing lines. All extreme sports need rules. Why are such rules necessary for kite surfers?

THINK ABOUT IT! Tom Atwell is a kite surfer. He said, "Your board going through water is like being on butter. It sounds like something sizzling on a grill." What do you think this quotation means? Connect it to what you know about kite surfing. Using his quotation as a model, think of another way to describe kite surfing.

SEE A DIFFERENT SIDE! Some places ban, or do not allow, kite surfing. They ban the sport for different reasons. Some places worry about safety. Others worry about the wildlife. For example, the U.S. Fish and Wildlife Service worries that kites and their shadows scare birds. Learn more about the perspectives of people who want to ban kite surfing. Do you agree? Why or why not?

Learn More: Resources

PRIMARY SOURCES

Over the Water, a documentary about the kite boarding career of Aaron Hadlow (2009).

Soul of Kite—Life of a Kite Surf Instructor, a documentary of Martin Kalmbach (2013).

SECONDARY SOURCES

Laval, Anne-Marie. *Windsurfing and Kite Surfing*. Mankato, MN: Smart Apple Media, 2013.

Timblin, Stephen. *Kitesurfing*. Mankato, MN: Child's World, 2012.

WEB SITES

International Kiteboarding Association: http://internationalkiteboarding.org

Professional Kiteboard Riders Association: www.prokitetour.com

United States Kiteboarding Association: www.uskite.com

Glossary

adrenaline (uh-DREN-uh-lin) energy

armada (ahr-MAH-duh) fleet, group of boats

canoes (kuh-NOOZ) little boats

footstraps (FUT-straps) straps on the board that secure feet to the board

hang time (HANG TIME) time spent in the air while doing a jump

harness (HAHR-nis) straps that secure a person to safety gear

icebergs (ISE-burgz) large, floating blocks of ice

inflatable (in-FLAY-tuh-buhl) can be pumped with air

inland (IN-luhnd) land that is far from oceans

landed (LAN-ded) achieved, completed

nautical (NAW-ti-kuhl) describing anything that has to do with sailing or ships

parachutes (PAR-uh-shoots) strong, light fabric attached to thin ropes that helps skydivers slow down their fall through the air

pier (PEER) a structure from beach out into water

shallow (SHAH-loh) not deep

towed (TOHD) pulled

Index